SandCastle

Word Families Set 7

-ore as in core

Amanda Rondeau

Consulting Editor Monica Marx, M.A./Reading Specialist

ABDO
Publishing Company

Published by SandCastle™, an imprint of ABDO Publishing Company, 4940 Viking Drive, Edina, Minnesota 55435.

Printed in the United States.

Credits
Edited by: Pam Price
Curriculum Coordinator: Nancy Tuminelly
Cover and Interior Design and Production: Mighty Media
Photo Credits: BananaStock Ltd., Corbis Images, Digital Vision, Eyewire Images, Hemera, PhotoDisc

Library of Congress Cataloging-in-Publication Data

Rondeau, Amanda, 1974-
　　　-Ore as in core / Amanda Rondeau.
　　　　　p. cm. -- (Word families. Set VII)
　　　Summary: Introduces, in brief text and illustrations, the use of the letter combination "ore" in such words as "core," "more," "snore," and "chore."
　　　ISBN 1-59197-267-1
　　　1. Readers (Primary) [1. Vocabulary. 2. Reading.] I. Title. II. Series.

PE1119 .R697 2003
428.1--dc21
　　　　　　　　　　　　　　　　　　　　　　　　　　　　　　　2002038206

SandCastle™ books are created by a professional team of educators, reading specialists, and content developers around five essential components that include phonemic awareness, phonics, vocabulary, text comprehension, and fluency. All books are written, reviewed, and leveled for guided reading, early intervention reading, and Accelerated Reader® programs and designed for use in shared, guided, and independent reading and writing activities to support a balanced approach to literacy instruction.

Let Us Know

After reading the book, SandCastle would like you to tell us your stories about reading. What is your favorite page? Was there something hard that you needed help with? Share the ups and downs of learning to read. We want to hear from you! To get posted on the ABDO Publishing Company Web site, send us e-mail at:

sandcastle@abdopub.com

SandCastle Level: Transitional

-ore Words

score

snore

sore

store

tore

wore

Jim wants to score a
goal.

Lila hears her dad
snore.

Tony has a sore throat.

Pat goes to the store
with his parents.

Buddy tore up the
newspaper.

Tara wore a red cap.

The Chore, the Snore, and the Sore

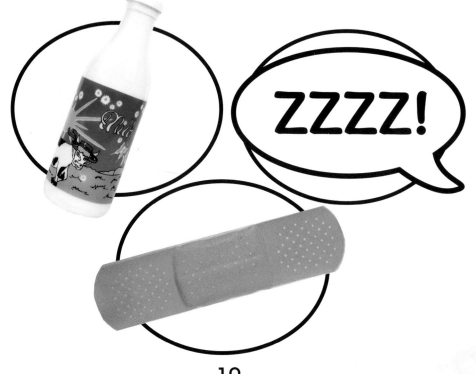

Every day Ben
had a chore.

He got milk at the store.

One day, on his way
to the store,

he heard a loud and
terrible snore!

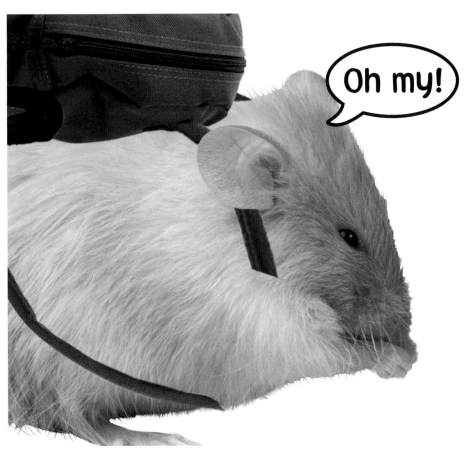

He had never heard this
by the store before.

Ben went in back
of the store to hear more.

He found a lion
whose paw was sore.

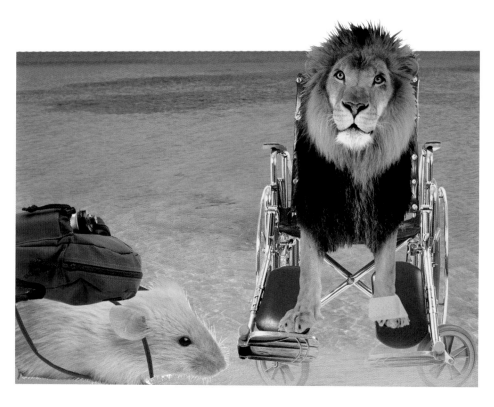

Ben helped the lion
to the shore.

He washed the paw
that was sore.

They became friends

forever more!

The -ore Word Family

before	score
bore	shore
chore	snore
core	sore
fore	store
gore	tore
lore	wore
more	

Glossary

Some of the words in this list may have more than one meaning. The meaning listed here reflects the way the word is used in the book.

chore   a regular job or task, like cleaning your room

goal   a point scored for getting a ball or puck to a specific zone

house   a building that people live in

parents   mothers and fathers

shore   the land at the edge of an ocean or a lake

snore   to breathe loudly when you are asleep

About SandCastle™

A professional team of educators, reading specialists, and content developers created the SandCastle™ series to support young readers as they develop reading skills and strategies and increase their general knowledge. The SandCastle™ series has four levels that correspond to early literacy development in young children. The levels are provided to help teachers and parents select the appropriate books for young readers.

Emerging Readers
(no flags)

Beginning Readers
(1 flag)

Transitional Readers
(2 flags)

Fluent Readers
(3 flags)

These levels are meant only as a guide. All levels are subject to change.

To see a complete list of SandCastle™ books and other nonfiction titles from ABDO Publishing Company, visit www.abdopub.com or contact us at:

4940 Viking Drive, Edina, Minnesota 55435 • 1-800-800-1312 • fax: 1-952-831-1632